Ladies gentlemenNew Egg

I0846415

Chap. 1 Lady Knight

The girl istoin the classroom, listening to the lesson boringlyeithern of the teacher. Suddenly, there is a scream and a crash outside the window.

The girl looks out and sees several zombies and other horrible creatures invading the school yard. The teacher tells the students to stay still and not to panic.tounique

hereYothere is a possible continuationeitherNo. of the story:

The girl can't believe what she sees. She feels that her hearteithern accelerates and fear invades her.¿ceitherHow is it possible that there are zombies and monsters in your school?¿Whatandhas passed?¿deitherwhere is itton the otherstos teachers and students?

She looks around and realizes that she is not there.toalone. There are other friendsñeros of class that alsoandn have seen the scene and it iston equally scared. Some cry, others scream, others hug each other. Nobody knows whatanddo.

The teacher tries to calm them down, but it is clear thatandhe tooandn esttohighly strung. He tells them that they have to leave the classroom and find a safe place. He tells them to follow his instructions and not to separate. He tells them to confYoin inandl.

But the girl didn't trustYoto inandl. She remembers that the teacher has always been very strict and boring. She thinks thatandHe has no idea about ceitherhow to deal with a situationeithern asYo. She thinks thatandHe is going to put them in danger.

AceYothat, when the teacher opens the classroom door, the girl takes advantage of the moment and runs in the directioneithern contrary. She wants to escape from school and find her family. She wants to survive.

The girl decides that she can't stay thereYowaiting to be devoured.

He grabs his backpack and runs out of the classroom, avoiding the zombies and other monsters. In the hallway, she meets a boy who alsoandn esttotrying to escape. The boy tells him to follow him, that he knowseitherwhere there is a way out.
The girl and the boy arrive at the school parking lot, where there is an abandoned car.

The boy tries to start the car, but he doesn't have the keys. The girl sees that there is a batandisbol in the back seat.

He takes it and tells the boy to use it to break the window and open the door. The boy does so, but in doing so, he sets off the car alarm.

Car alarm attracts attentioneithern of the zombies and the other monsters, who are heading towards them.

The girl and the boy manage to get into the car, but they can't start it. The girl tells the boy to look for somethingorUseful in the glove compartment or trunk.

The boy finds a gun and some bullets in the glove compartment. The girl tells him to pass it on, that she knows howeitherhow to use it.

The girl shoots the zombies and other monsters that approach the car, while the boy tries to make a bridge with the engine cables.
The girl manages to eliminate several enemies, but she runs out of bullets. The boy manages to start the car, but it has a flat tire. The girl tells him that it doesn't matter, he should drive anyway.

The girl and the boy manage to leave the school parking lot, but they find a street full of mtos zombies and mtos monsters.

The boy tries to avoid them, but the car is going very slow because of the flat tire. The girl sees that there is a sports store across the street. She tells the boy to stop thereYo, which maybetos they can find somethingorUseful to defend yourself and to fix the car.

The girl and the boy get out of the car and enter the sports store, closing the door behind them. Inside the store, they see various artYosporty asses that couldYoThey can still serve as weapons or tools.
The girl takes a large backpack and begins to fill it with what she finds: a bow and arrows, a knife, a rope, a brorjula, a whistle, a lighter, some bandages, some energy barsandticas and a bottle of water. The boy takes a wrench and a repair kiteithertire no.totics.

The girl and the boy leave the sports store, ready to continue their escape.

However, they encounter a group of armed soldiers who point their rifles at them. The soldiers tell them to identify themselves and give them everything they are carrying. The girl and the boy look at each other, not knowing whatanddo.

The girl and the boy do not fYoeven of the soldiers. They know that theandrcito istoinvolved in what istopassing and that they are not trustworthy. They think that the soldiers are going to interrogate them, rob them or kill them.

AceYothat, in an act of braveryYoOh clever, the girl tells the boy to play along. She pretends that she istoscared and that she is going to cooperate with the soldiers. She tells them their names███and Luis and who are students of the San José schooland. She tells them that they only carry some backpacks with clothes and food.

The soldiers relax a little upon hearing his words. They think they are stupidñThey are innocent and do not pose a threat. They tell them to check their backpacks and then leave them.ton go.

But when the soldiers approach them, the girl and the boy take advantage of the opportunity and take out some weapons that they hadYostill hidden in their backpacks. They shoot the soldiers and knock them out. Then, they run to a motorcycle that was parked nearby and get on it. They start the motorcycle and speed away, leaving behindtosa the wounded soldiers.

Further ahead they find another military group.

The girl decides that she is not going to be intimidated by the soldiers.

He tells them that they are the ones who must identify themselves and that they explain to them whatandits Ttogoing. The soldiers are surprised by the girl's attitude, but they do not lower their weapons. One of them tells him that they are part of a special unit sent to contain the paranormal outbreak that has turned people into zombies and other aberrations.

The boy asks the soldiers if there is anythingorn safe place they can go. The soldiers tell him that there is a military base nearby, where he iston evacuating survivors.

However, they warn them that the path istofull of dangers and that will haveton have to follow theireitherorders if they want to arrive alive. The girl and the boy agree to go with them, but they don't trustYostill completely in them.

The girl, the boy and the soldiers get into the car and start driving towards the military base. Along the way, they encounter several obstacles.toasses: barricades, burned cars, ditches, etc.
The soldiers use their weapons to make their way, while the girl and the boy help with what they can. The girl uses her bow and her arrows to shoot the zombies and other monsters that attack them from afar. The boy uses her wrench to fix the car when he breaks downYoto.

The girl, the boy and the soldiers arrive at the entrance to the military base, where there is a security checkpoint.

The soldiers show their IDs and allow them to pass.

Inside the base, they see several soldiers and civilians organized in differenttoareas: a hospital, a dining room, a warehouseandn, a workshop, etc.

The soldiers tell them what to assign themtoin a roomeitherwhere canton rest and then inform themton about the situationeithern.

The girl and the boy go to their roomeithern assigned, where there are two beds, a wardrobe and a table. The girl leaves her backpack on the bed and sits on it. The boy does the same in the other bed.

They both look at each other with exhaustion and relief. The girl tells the boy that she is called Lady Knight, because she likes to be strong and brave like a knight, but she alsoandn feminine and elegant like a lady.

The boy tells her that his name is Gentleman Lady, because he likes to be gentle and courteous.ands like a lady, but alsoandn masculine and adventurous like a gentleman.

The girl and the boy laughYobecause of their names that are so similar and so opposite at the same time.

They realize that they have a lot in common.orny who have saved each other several times.

They approach metos and they hug. They look into each other's eyes and kiss. At that moment, a noise is heard outside the room.eithern. Someone istoknocking on the door.

The girl and the boy separatetoask and they stand up.

The girl goes to open the door, while the boy stays behindtos of her.

When they open the door, they see one of the soldiers accompanying themNoto the base.

The soldier tells them that he has brought themYosome food and wants to talk to you about the missioneithern that they have to comply.

The girl and the boy invite the soldier to enter the room.eithern.

The soldier hands them a tray with some stosandwiches, some fruits and some drinks. He tells them to eat well, because they are going to need a lot of energy.Yoto.

He explains that the base istosurrounded by zombies and other monsters, and they have to find a way to eliminate them or escape from them.
The soldier ████ tells them thatandHe is part of a special unit that was sent to investigate what was happening in the city.

He tells them that they discovered that everything was part of a secret government experiment, which came outeitherevil and provocativeeitherthe liberationeithern of a virus that transformed people into zombies and animals into monsters.

He tells them that his missioneithern was to rescue the survivors and destroy the facilities where it originatedeitherthe virus.

He tells them that they managed to enter the base, but were attacked by a horde of zombies and other monsters.

He tells them thatandhe was theoronly one who survivedeitherand that he took refugeeitherin the bunker where I found themeither.

He tells them that the base has a self-destruct system.eithern, which is activated with a key thatandhe has.
He tells them that if they manage to reach the control center, they will be able toton detonate the base and kill all the zombies and monsters. He tells them that this is theoronly way to save yourself and the world.

He tells them that he istowilling to help them, but they need to trustandly follow youreitherorders. He tells them that they are hisoronly hope and they don't have much time.

The soldier tells them that there is a secret laboratory in the basement of the base, where it is believed that it originated.eitherthe paranormal outbreak.

He tells them that his missioneithern is to infiltrate the laboratory, find the source of the outbreak and destroy it. He tells them it's a missioneithern very dangerous.

The girl and the boy decide to accept the missioneithern, although they are afraid.

The soldier tells them to prepare, he will come outton in an hour.
He gives them special suits, helmets with communicators, glasses with vision.eithern night and some weapons mtos powerful. He tells them to put them on and wait for him in the parking lot. Then he leaves the roomeithern.

The girl and the boy put on the suits, helmets, glasses and weapons.

They look in the mirror and are surprised at how different they look. They tell themselves to take care of themselveston to each other and that confYoeven in their abilities. They kiss goodbye and leave the room.eithern.

The girl and the boy arrive at the parking lot, where it istothe soldier waitedtondolos.

The soldier tells them to get into an armored jeep, where there are two other soldiers.tos. He tells them that they are his friends.ñteam members and their names are Bravo and Charlie.

He tells them thatandhe is theYoder of the team and is called Alfa. He tells them to follow his instructions and not to ask questions.

The jeep leaves the military base and heads towards a secret underground entrance.

Alfa tells them that the laboratory istoto several kiloeithermeters deep and will haveton have to go through several levels of security.

He tells them that the laboratory istocontrolled by an artificial intelligence called Omega, which is responsible for the paranormal outbreak.

He tells them that Omega has access to all types of biological weapons.eithermagic, whatYomica and nuclear, and do not hesitatetoin using them to defend themselves.

The jeep reaches the secret entrance, where there is a door mettolica with a fingerprint reader.

Alfa gets out of the jeep and puts his finger on the reader.

The door opens and the jeep enters. The door closes behindtos of them.
Alfa tells them that he iston entering enemy territory and that they must be alert. He tells them that Omega knows that he iston ahYoand what will I dotoeverything possible to stop them.

The jeep moves along a tornel dark and narrow, where there are several ctomaras and sensors.

Alpha tells them that Omega istowatching your every move and can activate traps and ambushes at any time.

He tells them to trustYoin your instincts and you areandn prepared for anything. He tells them that the objective is to reach the laboratory control center, where they canton confront Omega and stop his evil plan.

The jeep stops in front of an armored gate, where there is a panel with a ceitherl say numberandrich.

Alfa tells them that they have to enter the ceitherl say right to open the hatch, but you don't know it.
He tells them that they have to look for clues in the tornel and solve a puzzle to get the ceithersay. He tells them to hurry, because Omega can send reinforcements at any time.

The girl and the boy get out of the jeep and begin to examine the tornel.

They find several sYoyn plungersormere writings on the walls, floor and ceiling.

AlsoandThey find remains of other vehiclesYoasses and soldiers who tried to enter before them.

Alfa tells them to radio and tell him what they see.

He tells them thatandl trytodecipher the riddle with the help of a computer porttouseful

The lady and the knight manage to solve the riddle and obtain the ceitherl say to open the hatch.

Alfa congratulates them on the radio and tells them to enter the ceitherl say on the panel. The lady introduces the ceitherl say and the hatch opens.

Alfa tells them to come intol ask and you laughornan withandl and the other soldiers in the jeep.

The lady and the knight enter the hatch and find a surprising scene.

The teaornel widens and becomes a large room filled with mtomachines, tubes, cables and screens.

Alfa tells them that he iston at level mtos high of the laboratory and that each level is mtos advanced and dangerous than the previous one.

He tells them that they have to go down to the m leveltos low, where istothe Omega control center.

The jeep starts up again and heads towards a ramp that goes down to the next level.

Alpha tells them to prepare to face the first obstacles.toasses

He tells them that Omega has created several mutant monsters with human and animal DNA, and has released them around the laboratory.

He tells them that they are very strong and aggressive, and that they have no mercy. He tells them to use their weapons carefully and not to waste ammunition.eithern.

The jeep goes down the ramp and reaches the second level of the laboratory, where there is a large cage with several mutant animals.

Alpha tells them that they are the failed experiments of Omega, who uses them as guards.

He tells them that they have to get through the cage undetected, or they will haveton have to fight against the beasts.

He tells them to wear their camouflage suits and follow their instructions.ñales.

The lady and gentleman put on their camouflage suits, which adapt to the color and texture of the surroundings.

Alfa makes them añwith his hand and tells them to follow him. The jeep silently slides through the cage, avoiding the mutant animals.

Some of them are mixes of lions, tigers, bears and wolves.

Others are mtos extrañyou, like serpents with wings, plowñace with tenttoasses and frogs with fangs.

The jeep manages to get out of the cage without being seen, but one of the mutant animals notices and starts roaring.

The other animals become alert and begin to chase the jeep. Alpha tells them to prepare to shoot.

He tells them to aim for the heads and hearts of the beasts, which are their target points.andbiles. He tells them not to be scared and to trustYoin his abilities.

The lady and the knight take out their guns and start shooting at the mutant animals that are chasing them. Some of them fall to the ground, but others keep moving forward. The jeep accelerates and moves away from the cage, but encounters a metal blockage. Alpha tells them that it is a trap by Omega, who has closed the exit. She tells them they have to find another way out or break the blockade.

- Sawñepisode 33: The lady and the gentleman see a hatch in the roof of the tornel, which seems to lead to another level. Alfa tells them that it is a possibility, but that he doesn't know whatandthere is on the other side. He tells them that they can try to climb through the hatch, but they will have toton have to leave the jeep and the other soldiers behindtos. He tells them that it is a decisioneithern diffYoeasy, but they have to do it rtol ask.

The lady and the gentleman decide to go up the hatch, thinking it is theiroronly optioneithern.

Alfa tells them that he supports them and that he will wait for them.toin the jeep

He tells them to take care of themselves and communicate when they get to the other side.
The lady and gentleman get out of the jeep and head towards the hatch, while shooting at the approaching mutant animals.

They reach the hatch and open it, revealing a metal ladder. They climb the ladder and close the hatch behindtos of them.

The lady and the gentleman arrive at the third level of the laboratory, where there is a large room full of zombies.

Alpha tells them over the radio that they are the remains of the humans that Omega infected.eitherwith a deadly virus.

He tells them that they are very dangerous and that they can infect them if they bite or scratch them.ñan. He tells them that they have to cross the room without making a sound, or he will haveton have to fight the zombies.

The lady and the gentleman take off their camouflage suits, which no longer fit them.

Alfa tells them to use their knives and silenced guns, which are mtos discreet than their rifles.
He tells them to stay together and cover each other's backs. The lady and knight move through the room, avoiding the zombies.

Some of them are soldiers, cientYofics and civilians who worked in the laboratory. Others are mtos extraños, such as infected animals, plants and objects.

The lady and gentleman make it to the other side of the room, where there is a door with a sign that says "Control Center."

Alfa tells them that they have reached theorlast level of the laboratory, where it istoOmega. He tells them to prepare for the final showdown.

He tells them that they have to enter the door and disable Omega, who istoconnected to a large computer. He tells them that it is hisorlast missioneitherny that they cannot fail.

The lady and knight enter the control center door, where they meet Omega. Omega is a bald man, with glasses and a white coat. He istositting in a chair, surrounded by wires and electrodes that connect him to the computer. Omega recognizes them and tells them that they are agents Alpha and Beta, the best in the agency. He tells them that he has been waiting for their visit, and that he wants to talk to them.
- Sawñeta 39: The lady and the gentleman point their guns at Omega, and tell him to surrender. Alfa tells them on the radio not to listen to him, that he is a madman and a traitor. Omega tells them that Alfa has lied to them, thatandHe is not the villain, but the handgnaw. He tells them that the virus he createdeitherIt is not to destroy the world, but to save it. He tells them that the virus is capable of evolving and adapting to any form of life, and that it can create a new humanity mtos strong and diverse.

The lady and the gentleman hesitate, and ask Omega whatandmeans.

Omega tells them what to show themtothe truth, and activate a boteithern.
On a giant screen, they look imtogenes from different places in the world, where there are people, animals and plants infected by the virus.

Omega tells them that these are his children, his creations.

He tells them that he has released the virus in several paYoses, and that will soon spreadtoall over the planet. He tells them that it is the beginning of a new era, the era of Omega.

The lady and the gentleman are shocked by what they see on the screen.

Alfa tells them on the radio not to be fooledñar, that Omega is a genocide and a monster.

He tells them they have to disconnect it from the computer and destroy the virus.

He tells them that it is their duty and their responsibility. The lady and the gentleman look at each other, and they don't know whatanddo.

Omega tells them not to listen to them, that Alpha is a tyrant and a coward.
He tells them thatandHe offers them freedom and diversity. He tells them to joinandhim, and that they are part of his new family.

He tells them that it is their opportunity and their destiny. The lady and the gentleman look at each other, and they don't know whatanddo.

The lady and the gentleman make a decisioneithern, and actoran.

¿Whatanddecideeithern taketon?¿It will be puttoOn the side of Alpha or Omega?¿Achieveton his missioneitherdo not changetoside?...

The lady decides to side with Alpha, and tells the knight that they have to fulfill their mission.eithern.

He tells him that Omega is crazy and a danger to the world.

He tells him that they can't let him continue with his plan.

The knight decides to side with Omega, and tells the lady that he is right.eithern.
He tells him that Omega is a visionary and a benefactor to the world. He tells her that they can't stop his work.

The lady and the gentleman point their guns at each other, and tell each other that they are sorry.

Alfa tells them over the radio that he can't believe what he is doing.topassing, and that begs you to reconsider.

Omega tells them on the screen that he istoproud of them, and congratulates them on their electioneithern. He tells them that it is the moment of truth, and that only one of them will emerge.toI live from thereYo.

The lady and the gentleman shoot at the same time, and wound each other. They fall to the ground, bleeding.

Alfa tells them on the radio that they are idiots, and that they have ruined everything.

Omega tells them on the screen that they are handroes, and that they have fulfilled their destiny.
He tells them not to worry, it will be soonton part of his new family. She tells them that she is waiting for them on the other side, and that she loves them.

The lady and the gentleman lie on the ground, unconscious.

Alfa tells them over the radio to wake up, that they can't leave him alone.

Omega tells them on the screen to go to sleep, it's over.ton at home.

Suddenly, an explosion is heardeithern, and the control center door opens. A group of soldiers enter, armed and equipped. They are the agency's reinforcements, who have arrived to finish off Omega.

The soldiers see the lady and the knight, and recognize them as their companions.ñEros.

They take them to a stretcher, and apply first aid. The soldiers see Omega, and point their weapons at him. They order him to log out of the computer, and for him to surrender.

Omega sees them, and isYoand. He tells them that they are too late, that the virus is alreadytoout of control.

He tells them that they can't stop him, that he is the master of the world.

The soldiers shoot Omega, killing him.

The computer shuts down, and the control center goes silent.

The soldiers believe they have accomplished their missioneithern, and they have saved the world. But they don't know that Omega hasYoto a contingency plan, and that thereYoHe has sent a copy of his mind to the cloud. Omega is still alive, and still controlling the virus.

Omega waits for the right moment to attack again, and to take revenge on those who betrayed him.

End of the Lady Knight.....

Chap. 2 Island

The alpha soldier, aka ████, he feels relieved and proud that he managed to detonate the base and destroy the virus.

ANDHe believes that he has done his duty and that he has saved the world.ANDHe communicates with his superior and informs him of hisandsuccess.

But his superior does not share his joy.Yoto.

ANDHe tells her there is bad news.
ANDHe tells her that ████, that the virus has not died.ANDHe tells her that █████ haveYoto a contingency plan.

ANDHe tells her that █████ He is still alive, and continues to control the virus.

ANDHe tells her that █████ has activated a second phase of his plan, and has released a new strain of the virus, mtoIt's lethal and contagious.

ANDHe tells her that the virus istospreading throughout the world, and it istoturning people into zombies and animals into monsters.

ANDHe tells her that the world istoon the brink of the apocalypse.

ANDHe tells her that there is good news.ANDHe tells her that they have located the source of theñat █████, and who know deitherwhere it is found.

ANDHe tells her that ███████ its Ttohidden on a secret island, where he has an underground laboratorytoneo.

ANDHe tells her that they have to infiltrate the island, find the laboratory and eliminate ████████ once and for all.

ANDHe tells her thatandhe is theoronly one who can do it.

ANDHe tells her thatandHe is the best soldier they have, and he trustsYoto inandl.

ANDHe tells her that he is going to assign her a new mission.eithern, and that he will send you a support team.ANDHe tells her to prepare to leave as soon as possible.

ANDHe tells her that this is hisorLast chance to save the world.

ANDHe tells her that she cannot fail.

ANDHe nods determinedly.eitherNy gets up from the chair.

He heads to the hangar where a helicopter is waiting for him.eitherblack ptero AllYoHe meets his support team: four agents who are experts in combat, infiltration,eithern, explosives and technologyYoto.

They greet each other with a gesture and board the helicopter.eitherptero.

The helixeitherptero takes off and heads towards the island, which istosurrounded by an anti-aircraft defense systemandrea.

The pilot informs them that he will haveton than parachuteYodas and land in a clear area.
He gives them headphones and glasses.eitherNocturnal
She tells them to keep in touch and follow the plan.

The SOS agent adjusts his equipment and prepares to jump. He looks out the window and sees the moonlit island.

feel a chillYoor when thinking about what awaits you thereYobelow.

Remember your boss's words: this is yoururorLast chance to save the world.

It cannot fail.
He throws himself into the voidYooday he feels the wind on his face.

Open the parachuteYoYou give and head towards the meeting point.

Go to your friendsñeros do the same. Hope everything turns out well.

He reaches the ground and takes off his parachuteYoyou give. I will beorne with their equipment and check their weapons.

They communicate through headphones and get going.

They have to infiltrate the island, find the laboratory and eliminate ███████ once and for all.

Documentationeithertarget number:

"The doctor is a scientistYocrazy girl she istoworking on a secret project to create a bioweaponeithermagic capable of destroying life on the planet.

Its Ttousing the island's laboratory as his base of operations, where he conducts experiments with viruses, bacteria, and mutant animals.

Your objective is to release the biol weaponeithergic in the world and cause a global pandemic.

She believes thatYocouldtopurify humanity and create a new superior race.

She is a cold womanYoa, calculating and ruthless.
He doesn't care about anyonetos that she herself and her visioneithern distorted science.

He has many enemies and allies, and does not hesitate to eliminate anyone who gets in his way.

The SOS agent and his team have to stop her before it's too late.

They have to infiltrate the laboratory, confront its guards and its creatures, and finish it once and for all."

The SOS agent's support team is called Team Alpha. Its Ttoformed by four agents who are experts in differenttoareas. Their names and specialties are:

- **Agent R**: It's himYoleader of the team and the person in charge of coordinating the actions. He is a veteran of several missions and has a lot of experience in the field. He is skilled in hand-to-hand combat and firearms. He has a serious and professional personality, but alsoandHe knows how to joke when necessary.

- **Agent L**: She is the infiltration specialisteitherny stealth. She is capable of entering and leaving any place without being detected. She is an expert at disguising herself, hacking security systems, and picking locks. She has a reserved and mysterious personality, but alsoandn is loyal and trustworthy.

- **Agent E**: He is the specialist in explosives and demolitions. He is capable of creating and defusing bombs, mines, grenades and other explosive devices. He is expert in causing mtoximo dañor with the mYomaterial mood. She has an outgoing and fun personality, but alsoandn is reckless and reckless.
- **Agent T**: He is the technology specialistYoae informtoethics. It is capable of handling any type of electronic device.eitherunique, from computers to drones. He is expert in creating and using gadgets, software and hardware. He has an intelligent and curious personality, but alsoandn is nerdy and sarctostic.

These are the members of the Alpha Team, the support team of the SOS agent.....

The Alpha Team command. of 5 men is sent to the island to recover and eliminate the sample of this virus in Dr. Cameron's laboratory.

When they finally reach a warehouseandn where it is believed that Dr. ███████ hides the (GPS) tracking of your virus, the device istomoving so the team decides to enter the warehouseandny make sure everything is going well.

Alpha Team approaches the warehouseandn cautiously.

Agent T uses his device to track the virus's GPS.

Tells them that the device istoinside the warehouseandn, but it moves from one side to the other. Agent R orders the team to prepare to enter.

He tells them that his goal is to recover and eliminate the virus sample, and not to leave anyorn trace.

Agent L is in charge of opening the warehouse doorandn with a hookorto.

Agent E places an explosive charge on the opposite wall, in case they need an exit.toask. Agent R and Agent SOS prepare to break into the warehouse.andn with their weapons ready.

Agent L opens the door and makes a gesture.ñto the rest of the team.

Agent R and SOS Agent enter first, followed by Agent L and Agent E.

Agent T stays outside, watching the perYometro and communicationtoconnecting with the team through headphones.
The warehouseandn esttodark and full of boxes, barrels and machinery.

The team advances carefully, searching for the virus's GPS.

Agent T tells them that the device istonearby, but cannot specify its locationeitherexact n. He tells them to be careful, there may be traps or guards.

Suddenly, a scream and a gunshot are heard.

The equipment is alerted and goes towards the source of the sound. AllYoThey find the SOS agent lying on the ground, bleeding from the chest. Next toandThere is a dead man, shot in the head.

He is one of Dr. Cameron's henchmen.

Agent R approaches the SOS agent and takes his pulse.

He tells him that he istoalive but needs attentioneithernmandsays urgent.

He tells him to resist, that they are going to get him out of there.Yo. The SOS agent looks at him with difficulty and tells him not to worry aboutandLet him continue with the missioneithern. He tells her that she has found the virus's GPS, and that she has it in her hand.

Agent R sees the device in the SOS agent's hand. It's a smallñto box mettolight with a flashing red light.

Agent R tells the SOS agent that he has done a good job, and that he is going to remove the device to complete the mission.eithern.

The SOS agent nods weakly and hands the device to agent R.

Agent R takes the device and examines it. He sees that he has a boteithern red and a digital display.

On the screen it says:"Activationeithern in 10 seconds". Agent R realizes that it is a trap, and that the device is a bomb.
Agent R yells at the rest of the team to get out of the warehouse.andn, it's a bomb. He tells them to throw away the device as soon as possible.tos far as possible and let them run.

The team reactstoask and leave the warehouseandn by the wall where Agent E livedYoThe explosive charge has been placed.

Agent R stays next to Agent SOS, who istounconscious. She tells him that she is sorry, but that she can't leave him alone. She tells him that she is going to die withandl, like a handgnaw.

He tells her that it has been an honor to work withandl.

The device starts beeping mtoMrtol ask, indicating that it is going to explode. Agent R hugs the SOS agent and closes his eyes. Wait for the end.

The bomb explodes, causing a large flare and shock wave. The warehouseandn jumps into the air, along with everything inside.

Alpha Team observes the explosioneithern from afar, shocked and sad. They have lost two of their friends.ñeros, and they have not been able to fulfill the missioneithern.

The doctor███████watch the explosioneithern from his laboratory, with an evil smile on his face. She has managed to deceiveñar to Team Alpha, and has escaped with the virus sample.

The doctor████████activates his final plan: release the virus into the world.

But it turns out that Agent R was an infiltrator of the Corporation.eithern"Three Steps", an organizationeithern criminal who sought to obtain the virus from the doctor████████to use it for evil purposesandfics.

Agent R habYoHe pretended to be a member of the Alpha Team, andYohas taken advantage of the trust of the SOS agent to approachandl.

Agent R habYohas sabotaged the virus's GPS device, and hasYohas become a bomb.

His plan was to blow up the warehouseandn, and fake his own death.....

AceYo, no one suspectYoto ofandhim, and will be ableYoto escape with the virus sample to getYoon your own.

But the SOS agentYohas been injured by an infected person, one of the doctor's experiments███████.

The infected person spoke to himYobitten him on the arm, and spoke to himYohas transmitted the virus.

The SOS agent has notYohas realized, and hasYocontinued with the missioneithern.

Agent R spokeYoHe noticed the wound, andYohas seen a golden opportunity.

Agent R habYoHe shot the infected person in the head, andYodropped next to the SOS agent.

AceYo, seemYobecause the infected person was the one who hadYoshot the SOS agent, and that agent R spoke to himYohas saved his life.
Agent R habYoHe pretended to care about the SOS agent, and spoke to him.Yohas removed the GPS device from the virus.

Then, thereYohas activated the bomb, andYoHe yelled at the rest of the team to get out of the warehouse.andn.

Agent R spokeYoHe stayed next to the SOS agent, and spoke to himYoto hugged

But it was not a gesture of friendship, but of betrayal.eithern.

Agent R spoke to himYoHe stuck a syringe in the SOS agent's chest, and told himYoto extraYotake a sample of your infected blood.

Then, thereYoHe has hidden the syringe in his pocket.

Agent R habYoHe closed his eyes, and spokeYohas waited for the explosioneithern. But he wasn't going to die with the SOS agent.

Agent R was wearing a bulletproof vest and a teleportation device.eithern.

In itorAt the last moment, before the bomb exploded, Agent R hadYoteleported out of the warehouseandn, with the virus sample in his possession.

Agent R spokeYoreunited with his ceitheraccomplices of the Corporationeithern"Three Steps", and I spoke to themYohas delivered the virus sample.

The Corporationeithern"Three Steps"there wasYomade him very happy, and I spoke to himYocongratulated for your work.

I spoke to himYoI have said that now you haveYoan advantage over the doctor███████, and what couldYocreate your own bioweaponeithergic.

Agent R spokeYoa satisfied sense of having been deceivedñadore Team Alpha, and having achieved their goal.

He didn't care about the world, nor about his former friends.ñEros. He only cared about money and power.

Now, as for the SOS agent, he had also been teleported, but in another location, although wounded in the chest, and his arm was infected with the virus, he managed to survive but his story is still uncertain.

The SOS agentYohas teleported to Maruata, a smallñto populationeithercoastal n of Mandxico, whereYohereYounconscious on the beach.

A group of fishermen hadYohas found and hasYotaken to a cabinñnearby, where I spokeYoThe wounds have healed.

The SOS agentYowoke up at nightYoNext, you feltandgoing extrañLove well.

It was habYoHe noticed that his chest and arm were completely healthy, with no apparent trace of the infection.eithern of the virus.

It was habYohas asked whatandI spoke to himYoto past,
and ceithermo habYohas reached thereYo.
The doctor's virus   It was a biological
weaponeitherlogic that I couldYoto alter the DNA of living
beings, dtogiving them supernatural abilities, but alsoandI
came backandmaking them crazy and violent.

The doctor   roomYohas escaped from the island
where he livedYohas carried out the experiment, and
hasYohas followed the trail of agent R and the
Corporationeithern"Three Steps".

She knowsYowhat do you haveYoyet to stop them before
they released the virus into the world, and caused a
catastrophe.tostrofe to his ideals of a perfect world.

The Corporationeithern"Three Steps"haveYoto evil plans
for the virus.

wantYoeven use it to create a new race of superhumans,
who would obey hiseitherorders without questioning
them.

Alsoandn wantYoeven eliminate all those who opposed
them, or who did not comply with their
standards.tostandards.

Agent R was one of his agents mtos loyal, and hoped to
receive a reward for his betrayal.eithern.

The Alpha TeamYoHe was shocked to discover that Agent R was an infiltrator.

It was habYostill felt betrayed and angry, and hadYoThey have sworn to take revenge.

Alsoandthere was noYostill worried about the fate of the SOS agent, who was his friend and companionñero.

I don't knowYowhether he was alive or dead, noreitherWhere was it?

just knowYoeven if you haveYostill have to find him, and stop the Corporationeithern"Three Steps"before it was too late....

End of CapYotitle 2.

Chap. 3 Dr. ████████

Dr. ██████ she was a brilliant scientistYofica who worked for an organizationeithern secret call"The order".

Their goal was to create a virus that could enhance human capabilities, and use it to create a new m society.tos advanced and fair.

Dr.▮▮▮▮▮roomYodedicated toñShe gave her life to this project, and she was convinced that it was the right thing to do.

a dYoa, an explosioneithern asoleitherto a city, and it was suspectedeitherwhat do you haveYoWhat to do with the virus.

A team was sent to recover samples and research data.eithern, and Dr.▮▮▮▮▮I was with them to analyze the site.

Upon arrival, they found a scene of horror: cadtomutilated buildings, burning buildings, and monstrous creatures attacking them. Dr.▮▮▮▮▮he realized it was a mutationeithern, due to radiationeithern eh ions...

Not onlyYohas improved human capabilities, but alsoandn the roomsYoto deformed and corrupted.

Dr.▮▮▮▮▮it felteitherguilty and horrified by what he hadYohas caused, and decidedeitherwhat do you haveYoto know in depth the cause....

However, his companionsñeros of"The order"they did not agree.

Dr. ███achievedeitherescape from the mutant creatures and take refugeeitherin an abandoned laboratory.

AllYofoundeithera computer thatorIt didn't work and connectedeitherto the network of"The order". wantYoto access the secret files that revealed the true propeitherradiation experiment siteeitherne ions, and quiandnes were responsible.

However, his attempt to hack the system did not pass.eitherunnoticed. One of his friendsñeros, Dr. Vega, realized what he was doing and sent himeithera message:

- Dr. ███, whatandits Ttodoing?¿whyandits Ttotrying to access informationeithern classified?¿He doesn't know that this is a betrayaleitherna"The order"?

- Dr. Vega, I need to know the truth. WhatandWhat did we do with our experiment?¿WhatandAre those creatures?¿Whatanddo we want to achieve with this?

- Dr. ▮▮▮▮▮▮▮, it's not your place to know that. You are only a hundredYofica, not a lYoright Your job is to follow theeitherorders and don't ask questions. Stop interfering with plans"The order"or will regretto.
- Dr. Vega, I'm not intimidated. I'm not going to stop looking for answers. I cannot ignore the horror we have created. I have to stop this, I have to find a cure.

- Dr. ▮▮▮▮▮▮, is inoruseful There is no cure for mutationeithern, there is only evolutioneithern. It is the destiny of humanity to become something higher, something mtos strong, something mtos powerful. You can't change that, you can only accept it or die.

- Dr. Vega, you aretocrazy. You don't want to improve humanity, you just want to control and destroy it. You are a monster, just like those creatures.

- Dr. ▮▮▮▮▮▮▮, you are naive, just like those humans dandbiles. You do not understand the greatness of our project, nor the honor of being part of it.andl.

You have made a serious mistake by rebelling against"The order". Now you will havetohave to face the consequences.

Dr. Vega cuteitherthe communicationeitherny activeeitheran alarm in the laboratory where Dr. ▮▮▮▮▮▮. Soon, several mutant creatures entered the place and pounced on her.

Dr. ▮▮▮▮▮▮Tomeithera gun that hadYofound and shoteitherto the beasts, but there were too many of them and they were very resistant. She realized that she was trapped and that she had noYoto escape.

Before the creatures reached her, she made aorlast thing: senteithera message to a friend of his who worked in another organizationeithern hundredYofic call"The resistance". I told himeithereverything you knowYoto about"The order"and the radiation experimenteitherne ions, and askedeitherto spread it to the world.

Then I closedeitthereyes and waiteitherits end.

AceYoends the story of the origin of the dr▮▮▮▮▮▮.....

End of Chapter 3.

www.ingramcontent.com/pod-product-compliance
Lightning Source LLC
Chambersburg PA
CBHW031434250726
48656CB00002B/981